Tried and Tested Strategies: Behaviour in the Early Years

Angela Glenn,
Jacquie Cousins and
Alicia Helps

 David Fulton Publishers

London

David Fulton Publishers Ltd
The Chiswick Centre, 414 Chiswick High Road, London W4 5TF

www.fultonpublishers.co.uk

First published in Great Britain in 2004 by David Fulton Publishers

10 9 8 7 6 5 4 3 2

David Fulton Publishers is a division of Granada Learning Limited, part of
ITV plc.

British Library Cataloguing in Publication Data
A catalogue record for this book is available from the British Library.

ISBN 1-84312-104-2

Typeset by Servis Filmsetting Ltd, Manchester
Printed and bound in Great Britain

CONTENTS

ACKNOWLEDGEMENTS

We would like to thank Tony Faulkner for his contribution and also for providing, with patience, much needed help and advice when technology refused to co-operate!

Thanks also to Linda Evans who has guided us through the process of writing this book and who continues to be a source of encouragement.

Thanks to Julia Clarke for drawing the illustrations.

INTRODUCTION

This book was written in response to requests for advice received from all sorts of people working with young children in a range of early years settings. Experience in delivering in-service training sessions and professional development courses has shown us that colleagues are looking for straightforward guidance in dealing with the challenges presented by many of the children they meet – particularly in matters concerning behaviour.

We have put together a range of common situations and suggested some 'tried and tested' approaches. There is no magic wand and these simple approaches will not always work. There will be children whose needs are more complex and who therefore need more expert intervention.

However, the majority of children will respond to consistent, 'firm but fair' handling with lots of praise and positive reinforcement.

As will be seen from the examples given, it can sometimes be very difficult to be clear about the causes of children's difficulties, but we do know that the child is trying to tell us something through his behaviour. He does not have the verbal skills of an adult and therefore we need to be sensitive to what it is that the child is attempting to communicate. This is easier said than done when the child is behaving very badly, but we hope this easily accessible book will be one

way of helping you to understand what the child is trying to tell you as well as providing practical ideas to deal with difficult situations. Sections 1, 2 and 3 of the book deal with some ideas and strategies that can be easily absorbed into the daily routine. Basically, good practice for children with special educational needs is good practice for all children.

It can be difficult to provide with any accuracy a 'diagnosis' for a child at the pre-school stage. We can't always differentiate between the child who has neurological difficulties such as autistic spectrum disorder (ASD) and the child who has symptoms of anxiety caused by emotional stress. Both children may develop repetitive and immature behaviour which makes them feel more secure, and both could present as being withdrawn and not responding to instructions.

When a referral to a specialist professional is made, however, it will be very useful if the practitioner concerned can offer accurate observations and details of the strategies that have/have not been successful. The pre-school setting can provide very useful information in advising the professional about social, cognitive and emotional aspects of the child's functioning. The checklists and recording forms provided in Appendix 1 will enable practitioners to keep track of what they see and what they do in an easy, accessible format.

(We have used the convention of referring to the child as 'him' and the practitioner as 'her' purely in order to avoid clumsiness in the text. This is not to suggest that children with behaviour difficulties are always boys, or that staff are always women.)

Ten tips for good behaviour management

- Adopt a simple and easy-to-follow behaviour policy and share it with all the staff, helpers and parents

- Keep lines of communication open with all concerned

- Involve parents/carers right from the beginning: be sensitive and offer support rather than recrimination

- Be factual when talking to parents/carers – opinions leave you open to having to justify yourself

- Keep a list of observations about the child's behaviour, i.e. what actually happens

- Remember to develop the child's strengths as well as tackling problems

- Focus on one particular behaviour at a time: behaviour difficulties can be very complex, but a small change in how you respond to a child can result in success on which you can build

- Concentrate on what is actually happening in your setting and over which you have some control. It is important to understand as much as possible about the child's home life but you have to accept that it may prove difficult to influence

- Be consistent

- Remember, there are no magic answers – what works for one child may not work for another

Good practice in seven simple steps

1. Be consistent

2. Use praise and rewards

3. Provide good models

4. Guide the child

5. Ignore bad behaviour

6. Remove from the scene

7. Apply sanctions

STEP 1
BE CONSISTENT

Start as you mean to go on and be calm, clear and consistent. Remaining calm and not 'mirroring' the behaviour of a child is a useful tactic when dealing with children who are, for example, having a temper tantrum. Reacting to attention-seeking behaviours in a cool, deliberate manner will have the effect of showing that you are displeased while not giving the child the kind of heightened attention he is seeking. If a child is throwing construction toys for instance, the adult might simply walk up to him, very quietly remind him of the rules and swiftly withdraw the toy as a consequence. Once the rules in your setting have been established and all staff members know how to deal with certain behaviours, it is vital that everyone responds in the same way. It is very difficult to backtrack once a precedent has been set. For example, if throwing sand is allowed to go unchecked one day, it will encourage children to keep testing the boundaries. As long as everyone knows the rules and how they are to be applied it will be much easier to be consistent. Children feel secure when they know and understand what the rules are and what is expected of them.

Mrs. Butler didn't say anything when I did this yesterday....

STEP 2
USE PRAISE AND REWARDS

This is the most effective way of reinforcing good behaviour. Always reward the child who tries to show he is succeeding and that succeeding is fun. Show the child how pleased you are.

Rewards can be all sorts of things – praise, hugs, smiles, stickers, stars, smiley faces, favourite activities, computer time, reading stories together, choosing time, certificates etc. How do you decide which to use? Using rewards is very much up to each individual setting. In some settings, it is policy to use only verbal rewards and to acknowledge rather than to praise wanted behaviours. Some children particularly like certain rewards, for example, being allowed extra time at a favourite activity, or a 'well done' sticker on their T-shirt. One of the most effective rewards is adult praise or acknowledgement. A simple 'I really liked the way you helped Jack to carry all those toys to the cupboard' can be very effective. Recognising achievements publicly is a powerful tool for raising self-esteem and motivation. Rewards do not have to be 'big' to have the desired effect. Varying rewards and changing them when they lose impact is important for maintaining motivation; one type of reward does not necessarily fit all children.

Five simple rules for rewards

1. Reward should be immediate, for example, if Jack has in the past been reluctant to tidy up and he is spotted helping to put things away, you could IMMEDIATELY say something like 'thank you Jack for doing such a good job and making things so tidy'.
2. Reward every time at first and less often when the child finds it easier. If the same reward is given when a child has become better at performing a particular task, the impact is lost. This will have the effect of diminishing motivation on the child's part.
3. Always praise the child when giving rewards.
4. Always say exactly why you're pleased with him. Instead of 'good boy' or 'well done', say 'I liked the way you waited for Luke to get off the slide before you went down. That was very sensible and grown-up.'
5. Reward children for all different types of good behaviour, so that every child has a chance of being rewarded (see p. 5 for ideas).

Praise

Use the child's name when praising him for doing the right thing. Children who behave badly often hear their names called out (their surnames too sometimes) but well-behaved children can go for days without hearing their name spoken out loud. If you see someone doing something helpful try saying

'Well done, Kayleigh. That was very kind of you/that looks very neat/etc.'
Some children really like to hear their name called for doing the right thing
and this may help to reduce the number of instances of bad behaviour. It also
lessens the likelihood that children will be labelled 'naughty Tommy' (to
distinguish him from 'reasonably well-behaved Tommy' and 'always well-
behaved Tommy').

Positive and specific comments

When praising a child for doing the right thing it is important that he knows
exactly what he has done right! Just saying 'Well done, Jamilla' may well
mystify some children (especially if they had just done something naughty
that you missed). It is far more effective to say, for example, 'Well done Jamilla
for sitting up so nicely,' or 'Well done Philip for lining up so sensibly' as this
will give a much clearer message not only to the target child but also to others
standing nearby. Note: children with very low self-esteem sometimes find any
kind of praise hard to handle. There can be occasions when adults have
commented enthusiastically on a child's painting only to find two minutes
later that they have scribbled all over it with black paint. These children need
very sensitive handling and may respond better if you praise a couple of
children together, e.g. 'Well done you two for painting such colourful
pictures', or 'Well done all of you who are playing in the sand so sensibly.'

Children can easily miss comments made to them, or questions asked of
them, especially if they are engaged in an activity. Saying their name first will
alert them: 'Rory ... Well done, you are getting on really well with your work.
Michael ... Why do you think the baby bear was crying?'

We can praise and reward children for:

Sharing

Turn-taking

Tidying up

Washing paint pots

Taking a message

Helping a friend

Showing kindness

Asking a good question

Giving a good answer

Putting on his own coat

Remembering to bring something from home

Noticing something interesting

Having a good idea

Being sensible

Being brave

Being patient

STEP 3
PROVIDE GOOD MODELS

Point out to the child someone who is doing well. Praise that person and encourage the child to do the same. Always try to show the child the behaviours you want by commenting when other children are doing the right thing: 'I can see someone sitting very still, listening carefully and looking at me. Well done Sara.'

When sharing stories use the characters to share ideas with the child about good and bad behaviour: 'What do you think about Roger not taking his turn to help set the table?' (*It's Your Turn, Roger!* by Susanna Gretz published by Red Box).

Use the home corner to model good behaviour: 'Thank you for the cup of tea Ben. You have been so kind to me. Let me do the washing up for you.'

Use puppets to demonstrate good and bad behaviour: 'Susan was very naughty to take the biscuit from Teddy. Teddy is crying now and doesn't want to play with her any more. Let's bring on Kind Kelly to show Susan how to share with friends. Kelly has lots of friends – why do you think everyone likes to play with her?'

STEP 4
GUIDE THE CHILD

For example when clearing away, show the child step by step and expect him to do it in a similar sequence: 'Well done Tom, you've sorted out the wax crayons from the pencils. Now let's put the crayons into the red box and the pencils into the tub. Then we can put everything away in the cupboard.'

Help the child to succeed by breaking up tasks into smaller, achievable steps and praise at each stage. For example, if a child has difficulty sharing toys and pushes others away when they attempt to play, you could at first only expect him to play a simple interactive game such as rolling a ball to another child with adult supervision and then perhaps gradually increase the time and numbers in the group. By introducing different activities and turn-taking in a very small group at first and rewarding each success you can build upon achievements in a positive manner.

Giving a child take-up time can also help. If you ask a child to do something, particularly if it is something they do not really want to do, it helps if you do not stand over him and watch. Give him some space and take-up time and he may well comply without you even having to repeat the instruction. A really big egg timer can also help when you want a particular activity to stop. Advance warning of changes of activity is beneficial in reducing conflict, for example: 'When the sand has gone through I would like you all to be sitting on the carpet/have your coats on.'

When choosing is required, use limited choices such as 'Would you like to play with Lego or the cars?' If too many choices are presented it could encourage lack of focus and 'flitting'. The most difficult times of the day/session for children with behavioural difficulties are the unstructured times, e.g. free choice and outdoor play. It is during these particular times that the child will need the most direction and support. You could try helping him to plan for himself what he wants to do first – explain the choices and remind him exactly how you expect him to behave: 'We are going outside now Simon. You could ride on the trike or play on the slide – which one will you choose? If you play on the trike, remember to go round the other children so that you don't bump into them. If you play on the slide, you have to let other children have a go as well, so climb up the steps and slide down when it's your turn. If you stand on the steps all the time, the other children can't have a go.' You may need to repeat the expectation once Simon has chosen his activity and is actually on the equipment.

Plan what you will do with a child who finds it very difficult to move about the setting in an appropriate way. If you are moving from one room to another, support the child by having an adult walking next to him giving prompts or even holding his hand, and modelling the expected behaviour. Praise him if the behaviour is achieved.

STEP 5
IGNORE BAD BEHAVIOUR

Ignore irritating behaviour whenever possible and always try to avoid confrontation. It is often best to ignore the child's behaviour if it is annoying but not too severe, for example, a child constantly calling out. Ignoring means not giving any attention and pretending the behaviour is not affecting you at all. Make it clear to the child before the story time or circle time session that he will have a special reward when the story or circle time is finished if he has managed to sit quietly. (Be warned that initially the child's behaviour is likely to become worse as he struggles even harder to get what he wants, especially if he is seeking attention. You have to ignore him every time and make sure he doesn't receive attention from anyone else.)

Tactical ignoring can also avoid drawing everyone's attention to the unwanted behaviour. For instance, if a child is quietly staring into space and not following your instructions, there is no point in saying 'Stop daydreaming David.' All that happens then is that everyone near David stops what they are doing to look at him and instead of one child off task you have a whole group. A far more effective strategy is to say: 'Well done Leah and Daisy for tidying up.' Quite often Leah and Daisy will tidy up even more quickly and happily and with luck, David will stop daydreaming and help too. Similarly, giving out some new crayons or pencils to a group of children actively engaged in a task can be a real incentive to others to settle down and join in.

A lot of children react badly to the word 'No' and have learnt that engaging adults in a lengthy argument will often result in the adult giving in for the sake of a quiet life (the alternative being a major wobbly at the checkout!). By saying 'Yes, when …', rather than 'No, because …' you can reduce the likelihood of confrontation. For example, if a child wants to play with the Lego but needs to wash the paint off his hands first, try saying, 'Yes, when you've washed your hands, then you can play with the Lego' rather than 'No, because you've got dirty hands.'

Similarly, if a child is in the wrong place doing the wrong thing, for example, splashing others by the sink rather than sitting listening to a story, try asking him 'What are you supposed to be doing?' rather than 'Why are you doing that?' 'Why?' questions tend to get in response either a blank stare, one of those irritating shoulder shrugs or an obviously true answer such as 'Because I like splashing water around.' The 'What are you supposed to be doing?' question, or 'Can you remember what I asked you to do?' should elicit a more suitable answer.

STEP 6
REMOVE FROM THE SCENE

Removing the child from the situation and giving him some 'time out' can prevent escalation of the problem and allow him a 'cooling off' time out of sight of the other children. As always, announce 'time out' in a calm voice and reserve it for more serous misdemeanours such as aggression, violence, destructiveness or repeated rudeness.

Time out should be for the minimum possible time – a few minutes are as effective as a longer period. A useful guide is to consider the age of the child. A three-year-old could have a three-minute time-out period. An egg timer could be used to measure this. It should not be a humiliating or scary experience for the child but more a chance to calm down and return to the room to make a fresh start, hopefully with an apology if this is appropriate. Someone should stay with the child and sit close to him, but be careful not to reward with an activity he likes doing or making him too comfy in the staffroom for example. Think carefully about what to call the time-out place: the 'peaceful cushion', or the 'quiet place' or the 'calming corner' has more positive connotations than the 'naughty corner'!

STEP 7
APPLY SANCTIONS

Use sanctions only as a last resort. Taking away privileges such as choosing time or a special activity can be powerful in making a point with a child, but may well be counter-productive if he feels embittered about it. With children whose parents frequently use sanctions as a punishment, the impact will be minimal. If you do decide to take this route, make sure the child remembers why this is happening, especially if there has been a time lapse: 'Darren,  you won't be having a go on the computer today because you kicked Iqbal and made him cry. I know you like to play on the computer so I hope you will be kind to everyone in nursery tomorrow and then you can have your turn.'

Remember – rewards are much more effective than sanctions so **catch the child being good.**

SOME ADDITIONAL IDEAS

Noise levels

Many children have only two setting on their volume control – VERY LOUD and EVEN LOUDER. Letting off steam and shouting while playing outdoors is very different from doing the same thing indoors with lots of others; some children will need to be shown the difference between an indoor voice and a playground or outdoor voice. It is vital that the adults also demonstrate the difference and refrain from shouting across the room to each other or talking to each other while everyone is supposed to be watching a video for example. A **noisometer** could be positioned on the wall (like a thermometer) with a movable arrow that can be pointed to 'Just Right', 'Getting a Bit Loud' and 'Far Too Noisy'. A traffic light indicator might also be used. One successful strategy is to use a puppet or soft toy which goes into hiding if it gets too noisy and only comes out for a cuddle when things have quietened down again. This seems to work for all ages of children.

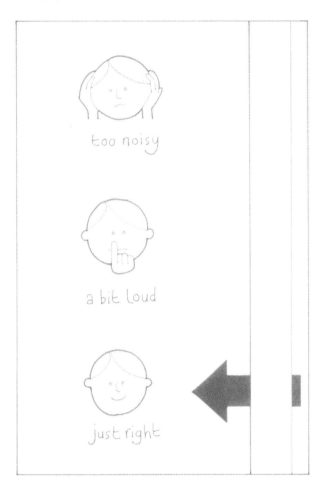

NOISOMETER

too noisy

a bit loud

just right

Chairs

If you are reading a story with the children sitting on the carpet in front of you it is very tempting to tell a fidgety child who is getting on everyone's nerves to go and sit on a chair. Although this gets him out of the situation and stops him irritating others, there is a fundamental problem with this strategy. By giving the badly behaved child a chair to sit on – which, let's face it, is a lot more comfortable than sitting on a hard floor – we can be seen to be rewarding unwanted behaviour. Try giving the child his own 'sitting spot', a square of carpet or material or a chalk-drawn shape.

Be alert to children becoming uncomfortable – allow them to get up, move about, have a stretch then settle down again. Young children should not be expected to sit still for long periods of time – it's difficult enough for adults!

Playing outdoors

Some children are reasonably well behaved indoors but get completely out of hand in more open spaces, barging into others and spoiling their games. It may be worth considering some form of 'passport' which they give to the outside supervisor who puts a smiley face on the passport if they have a good playtime. Five smiley faces result in a special certificate, star or choice of favourite activity. Teaching children how to play simple games can help with problems like this (Oranges and Lemons, Old Macdonald, What's the Time Mr Wolf?) and getting them to run round (all the same way) for a few minutes helps to burn off excess energy.

Rules

If your setting has some clearly displayed and easily understood rules you can save a lot of unnecessary dialogue by simply repeating the rule. If a child is swearing or shouting, rather than admonishing him you can say: 'We speak kindly', or 'We play carefully and safely.'

In brief:

- Make sure rules are known and understood by the children, parents and all staff – revisit them often

- Use a home–school liaison book for positive behaviours/achievements to share with parents/carers and in the setting

- Use a high degree of structure for children with behaviour problems

- Give responsibility to children with behavioural difficulties, for example by appointing them as the helper at snack time

- Use favourite activities as rewards

- Use visual aids wherever possible, e.g. if giving instructions about washing hands, show a picture of the children using the wash area

- Use a personal carpet square or 'spot' for children who have problems sitting still for a story

- Use a variety of rewards and change them when they lose impact

- Use extension activities – keep a box of resources ready and add to it over time

- Make sure children know what you mean if you have to tell them off. 'Stop that' is not enough – 'Stop throwing sand' will send the message to all the children

- Following a request, say 'thank you'; this implies that the request will be carried out

Quick tips for establishing good relationships

- Be positive and generous with praise

- Be careful how you talk to people. It is much better to say 'You will find it easier if ...' rather than 'Don't do it like that.' Remember, an unkind word lingers much longer than a kind one

- Label the act NOT the child, e.g. 'Pushing Fred was a dangerous thing to do', rather than 'YOU are a bully'. Negative labels stick

- Build in success. Make sure that programmes of work enable all children to succeed in some way

- Think back. Remember your own schooldays? Teachers are the creators of memories – make sure that your setting is a happy one. Do not be afraid to have some fun

- Smile. Non-verbal messages are important to children. A pat on the back, a smile, a nod gives as much encouragement as words

- Children often have the answer. After an incident, ask the child, 'Why might I be angry now?' Encourage children to analyse their own behaviour and begin to take responsibility for it

Quick tips for raising self-esteem

- Celebrate children's differences and unique personalities – don't expect every child to behave/respond in the same way

- Find something to praise in every child, every day

- Look at every child – establish eye contact as often as possible

- Make time to listen to children as well as talk to them

- Take their feelings seriously by noticing and acknowledging feelings whether good or bad

Things to say:
'I expect you are feeling ... now'
'That must be upsetting ... do you want to tell me about it?'
'You seem ...'
'You look ...'

Real children in real settings: behaviours that cause concern and strategies for coping

CASE STUDIES

1. A quiet, withdrawn child
2. A child demanding constant adult attention
3. A child who screams when asked to participate in an adult-led activity
4. A child who kicks children and adults
5. A child with a very short attention span
6. A child who has temper tantrums
7. A child who is oppositional
8. A child who refuses to talk (selective mute)
9. A child who is unable to share
10. A child who has difficulty turn-taking
11. A child who may have autistic spectrum disorder (ASD)
12. A child who is aggressive
13. A child who scribbles on other children's drawings
14. A child who scribbles on her own drawings
15. A child who constantly says 'No'
16. A child who makes himself sick
17. A child who runs out of the room
18. A child who hides under the table
19. A child who self-injures
20. A child who swears
21. A child who takes her clothes off
22. A child who spits
23. An over-affectionate child
24. A child who constantly tells lies
25. A child who always has to be 'first'
26. A child who bites

CASE STUDY 1

A quiet, withdrawn child

William spends much of his time at pre-school in the book area on his own. He watches the other children but will not respond when they try to talk to him. He hides his face and looks the other way when children try to talk and play with him. Most children now leave him on his own.

Possible reasons for this behaviour:

- Shyness – it may be a part of William's personality
- Does William get attention at home for this behaviour?
- Difficulty with understanding language
- Difficulty with social skills; William may not have had a lot of social contact before joining pre-school and needs time to adjust to a busy environment
- Withdrawn behaviour may indicate some more serious underlying problems at home if it persists over several weeks in spite of appropriate responses by staff

Strategies:

- Avoid pressurising him – he may need time to settle and just watch for a while, joining in when he is ready
- Talk with parents/carers and find out how William behaves at home. A home visit can often tell you a great deal
- Check that his hearing is not impaired
- Encourage William to play with one child initially, alongside each other with Lego (or similar). Gradually introduce some co-operative element such as building a fort together
- Monitor William's behaviour when on his own or when encouraged by an adult, to find out what he enjoys doing
- Praise him whenever he is with other children
- Introduce a 'special friend' for the day who will help William to join in with activities
- (Add your own ideas here)
-
-
-

CASE STUDY 2

A child demanding constant adult attention

As soon as Tara comes into pre-school she seeks an adult and will not leave her mother until she is holding the hand of another adult. She will only play or do activities when an adult is near her and constantly looks out for adults. Whenever she does a puzzle she looks at the adult before she puts the pieces in the slots. When the adult moves away she will just sit and do nothing or watch for the adult coming back.

Possible reasons for this behaviour:

- Coming into a new environment and feeling insecure is the primary reason for this sort of behaviour. It is important to be patient and allow enough time for children to feel at home with new surroundings and unfamiliar people
- Adults at home have done most things for her and not encouraged independence
- She is the youngest in the family where she is treated as 'the baby' and wants to maintain this level of attention
- Receptive language difficulties – not understanding what adults are saying and therefore unsure about what she should be doing

Strategies:

- Find out about the family situation and try to work out a simple plan to encourage independence at home. For example, the first emphasis could be on Tara attempting to do a puzzle or play with a toy by herself. She should be praised every time an adult notices her trying to do this on her own
- Implement an intensive praise and reinforcement schedule so that Tara begins to recognise all the good things she is doing. Initially it will be important to praise Tara for every single thing she attempts and draw her attention to the way she is progressing. In this way she will gain self-confidence
- Design a specific programme for Tara coming into the pre-school. When she is greeted by an adult worker she could then be introduced to another child and the two children could be encouraged to play with something they enjoy or to share a story together

- Work out a simple recording system so that Tara and her parents/carers become aware of how she is progressing. A simple star or sticker chart will serve as a record of how many times Tara has tried to do things on her own – but be aware that stickers do not work as a reward for *all* children

-

-

-

-

CASE STUDY 3

A child who screams when asked to participate in an adult-led activity

Most of the time, Kieran really enjoys pre-school. He is a lively boy with lots of friends and loves the big equipment such as the slides and scooters. He is very happy playing with things he enjoys. The problem starts when he is asked to do some table-top activities. He starts to scream really loudly so that many children stop what they are doing. This can go on for about 15 minutes.

Possible reasons for this behaviour:

- This is learnt behaviour from home – if he screams for long enough he will get what he wants
- He is attention seeking and knows that if he screams people will watch him
- He has difficulty with some table-top activities and does not like seeing other children doing things better than him. He is afraid of failure. He has difficulties with following instructions

Strategies:

- Remove any audience if possible and ensure the other children are engaged in their own activities. If you have an area or another room available move the other children away leaving one adult to watch over Kieran
- Encourage Kieran to sit in a quiet area until he is ready to join in. This needs to be explained to him before any screaming sessions start so that he is aware that he can have some time to think about what he is doing
- Use a visual timetable so that Kieran can choose his own activities for the session but ensure that he understands that he must include at least one table-top activity. In this way he is becoming involved in making his own choices but with the understanding that it includes a range of activities
- Use a visual timetable on which the order of events is clearly displayed. Kieran can then finish each section before moving onto the next section
- Reward him on any occasion that he does co-operate with table-top activities
-
-
-
-

CASE STUDY 4

A child who kicks children and adults

Dominic enjoys the big toys at pre-school. He likes the slide and playing chasing games with two other boys. If he is asked to come along to a table-top activity and he does not want to he will kick out at the pre-school worker and refuse to go. If he wants to play with a particular toy and other children will not let him, he will kick those children and also bite them. He has been known to bite adults.

Possible reasons for this behaviour:

- Dominic has learned that he gets to do things he wants to when he kicks and bites
- Dominic has had no models of sharing and insufficient positive experience of sharing
- He does not consider the feelings of others and finds it difficult to respond to meaningful social situations

Strategies:

- Dominic will need praise whenever he plays well with other children and responds to adult requests ('Well done Dominic, I like the way you waited for Sean to get off the trike – isn't he kind to let you have a go.')
- There will need to be clear rules in place at pre-school so that Dominic is fully aware of expectations of his behaviour. These rules will need to include how to relate to other children when they are playing with toys and how to ask them politely if he wants to play with a toy they have. Some stories and (puppet) role play may prove useful
- Dominic will need to learn that kicking and biting is unacceptable behaviour and clear consequences should be in place for when he does bite or kick. It will be important that he does not receive additional adult attention for his biting or kicking
- Dominic may benefit from specific sessions to teach social skills such as turn-taking and sharing equipment. These could be carried out in small groups focusing on a specific theme such as when a child wants to play with a toy that someone else has. Role play would be helpful
- Keep pointing out children who are playing nicely and who are able to share toys so that Dominic becomes fully aware of what is expected of him
-
-
-
-

CASE STUDY 5

A child with a very short attention span

Rehanah cannot sit still and listen to a story at story time. She constantly shuffles about on her hands and knees disturbing the children around her. She does not seem to notice that other children are trying to listen to the story. She constantly shouts out and interrupts the story and tries to talk about irrelevant things.

Possible reasons for this behaviour:

- Little experience of listening to stories and group situations
- Hearing difficulties
- Attention seeking
- Receptive language problems: understanding of language. Rehanah may not understand every word in a sentence when being spoken to; she may only understand one or two key words, making stories very difficult to follow
- Social awareness difficulties: Rehanah may have difficulty with the social rules of behaviour, e.g. not butting in when others are talking
- Very immature behaviour which could be a reflection of her general cognitive abilities

Strategies:

- Give her a special place to sit such as on a cushion and let her hold a special toy so that 'Teddy' can listen to the story too. Initially, expect Rehanah to sit for a short length of time such as three minutes with an adult nearby. Gradually the time can be extended and the adult can move farther away. If she manages to sit still for the required time, then give her a reward
- Suggest to her parents/carers that they arrange for an eye test and/or hearing test via the GP. If the behaviour continues despite clear expectations and a carefully structured behaviour plan, it may be helpful for her to sit near an adult reading the story so that she can see the pictures more clearly or be more involved in the process by helping to turn the pages over. In this way she will be given special responsibility and can be praised
- Give praise whenever Rehanah is sitting still and looks as if she is listening so that she receives attention whenever she is being 'good'. She may need to be shown very clearly what 'being good' is. When possible ignore her shuffling
- Point out children who are sitting nicely and listening so that Rehanah is clear about expectations. It can be helpful to remind children before

the story of the way to listen: 'Bottoms on the floor, lips together, eyes looking at me' – with appropriate gestures. Try asking them a specific question at the beginning. In this way they are listening out for something specific in the story telling

- Let Rehanah become accustomed to listening to stories by sitting in a small group or one-to-one with an adult so that she gets used to listening to the whole story. Start with very short stories. Stories recorded on tape and heard through headphones can be useful
- Praise her whenever you see her sitting still
- Have a clear system in place for whenever Rehanah is causing disruption such as sitting her on her own away from the group with a book
- Use a real photograph (with parents' permission), of Rehanah sitting still to act as a prompt: 'Look Rehanah, here you are sitting very still. I hope you will be sitting like this while I read the story today'
- Monitor her rate of learning. If she has difficulty in naming colours, learning simple rhymes, constructing simple phrases, the inattentive behaviour may be part of a general learning difficulty
-
-
-
-

- Have detailed knowledge of their child's progress through developmental stages
- Have important information about early health and developmental checks and will be able to provide details of contacts with other professionals, e.g. speech and language therapists, physiotherapists etc.
- Have problems and difficulties of their own – be understanding and realistic in your expectations
- May lack confidence in playing out their role – give them encouragement and practical support

What do we mean by 'parental responsibility'?

It is important that professionals understand who has parental responsibility for a child. The Children Act 1989 uses the phrase 'parental responsibility' to sum up the collection of duties, rights and authority that a parent has in respect of a child. In the event of family breakdown, both married parents will retain parental responsibility even if they then live in different households. In relation to unmarried parents, only the mother will have parental responsibility unless the father has been granted parental responsibility by the court or a parental agreement has been reached with the mother. Where a residence order is in place in respect of a non-parent (e.g. grandparent), that person will have parental responsibility for the duration of the order.

If a child is 'looked after' by a local authority, he may either be on a care order or be voluntarily accommodated.

First point of contact

The pre-school is often the parents' first point of contact with the education system. Remember that you are laying the foundations for effective partnership for the next 16 years or so. A negative experience with staff in the pre-school setting can sour a parent's attitude to 'teachers' for the rest of the child's school life – especially if the parent had a less than enjoyable time at school.

When there is concern about a child's behaviour, parents should be fully involved in the pre-school-based response for their child. The purpose of any intervention or programme of action should be explained carefully to them and they should be told about the local parent partnership service.
- Pre-schools must tell parents when they first identify that a child has SEN
- Pre-schools should keep records of their discussions with parents from when they first identify that a child has SEN. These records should be brief, recording key information given and parents' opinions in a standard format (an example can be found in Appendix 1)

Communication

To make communication with parents and carers effective, pre-schools should:
- Acknowledge and draw on parental knowledge and expertise in relation to their child
- Recognise the personal and emotional investment of parents and be aware

of their feelings – focus on the child's strengths as well as areas of additional need

- Ensure that parents understand procedures, are aware of how to access support in preparing their contributions and are given documents to be discussed well before meetings
- Respect the different views people may hold about an issue and seek ways to ensure all views are heard and recorded
- Respect the differing needs of parents themselves, such as a disability or communication and linguistic barriers
- Recognise the need for flexibility in the timing and structure of meetings
- Provide a comfortable and welcoming area for meetings
- Encourage parents to 'bring a friend' to meetings if they would find this helpful
- Make sure the meeting has an agenda and a realistic time limit
- Keep meetings friendly but business-like
- Be prepared to make home visits
- Define routes of referral to other sources of information and support
- Make sure written reports are as jargon-free as possible
- Ensure that parents are aware of an IEP, understand the targets and that everyone is working consistently to support the child

Pre-schools working in partnership with parents

- It is vital that pre-schools welcome and encourage parents to participate from the outset and throughout their child's time at the pre-school
- Pre-schools need to regularly review their policies to ensure they encourage active partnership with parents and do not present barriers to participation
- Pre-schools should seek to actively work with their local parent partnership service

Transition to school

Pre-schools are now being asked to perform much like reception teachers with regard to planning the curriculum, planning for children with special needs and record keeping. In theory, this should make liaison with schools easier. A uniform approach to record keeping and the ability to produce useful information is a big step towards the recognition pre-schools deserve. Now that early years settings are mentioned in the Code of Practice, recording for children with SEN has become more important. The recording pack in Appendix 1 will give a guide to the kind of records that pre-school settings and schools will find useful.

Pre-school staff should feel comfortable about setting up liaison procedures with the schools to which their children will move on. A discussion between the SENCOs about a child can make a lot of difference to the settling-in period. Pre-school staff should feel confident about passing on vital information. Confidentiality is often an issue, but most parents will be comfortable with the idea of SEN records being passed on to the school. It should be made clear that if schools know well in advance about children coming to them, they will be in a position to make the best possible provision for those children. Schools' SEN budgets are usually set in the spring term for the following autumn term, so the pre-school will need to make contact with a school well in advance.

Some schools and pre-schools have good liaison and transfer procedures. If you are concerned that you do not have a satisfactory transfer system, ask the school SENCO to visit or to meet you to discuss this. Some schools have set times for the children in the pre-school to make visits when they can see their classroom and meet their teacher, find out where the toilets are, where they will have their lunch, what the playground and toys are like, and where they will hang their coats – all the practical things which tend to worry children going to school.

For some children with more complex special needs, it may be advisable to make more visits and for their support worker to accompany them as appropriate.

Most children really look forward to going to 'big school' but there are some who find the prospect of leaving the familiar surroundings of their pre-school unsettling. If there are good systems in place for liaison and transfer it will ensure that the move for those children is as stress-free as possible. The more parents know about the procedures the better as they will be reassured that their child is being introduced to the next stage in their education in the best possible way.

Tips for easy transition to school

- Make sure you have parental consent before forwarding SEN records
- Set up informal and formal liaison procedures with all the schools you 'feed'
- Get to know the school staff – especially the SENCO – so that the procedures above become more comfortable
- Ask about making visits to school with the child/children
- Keep brief records and information to pass on (IEPs etc. see Appendix 1)
- Tell the children well in advance about the move into school and discuss regularly in a positive way
- Try to keep a professional distance – you can only be responsible for what the child does in your setting so try not to worry about how he will cope when he leaves you. It is absolutely natural to think about how children will cope when they are in school, especially those you may have been supporting closely, but it is worth remembering that schools have well-established procedures in place to support children with SEN

By following the steps outlined above, you can be confident that you have done all you can to 'smooth the way' for every child in your care to make the transition to school as happy as possible.

APPENDIX 1

Recording pack

SEN register

Observation sheet

Observation sheet example

IEP blank

IEP Rehanah

IEP William

IEP tracking sheet

Meeting with parents/carers

Special Educational Needs Register

Name of setting:			SENCO:	
Date:				

Child's name	DoB	Stage SA or SA+	Key worker	Date added to/ taken off register

OBSERVATION SHEET

NAME:	DoB:	DATE:

PRE-SCHOOL:

REASON FOR OBSERVATION:

TIME:	**OBSERVATIONS**: record the context of the behaviour (the activity going on, people present etc.), the possible trigger for the behaviour (what happened immediately before), the exact behaviour itself – just as it happened (what you saw, not what you think about it).

ACTION:

OBSERVATION SHEET

NAME: Brendan	DoB:	DATE:

PRE-SCHOOL:

REASON FOR OBSERVATION: Ricky's mum has complained that he has been getting upset about coming to nursery because he says that Brendan punches him.

TIME:	OBSERVATIONS: record the context of the behaviour (the activity going on, people present etc.), the possible trigger for the behaviour (what happened immediately before), the exact behaviour itself – just as it happened (what you saw, not what you think about it).
10.30	Outside playtime. Weather is fine, so children have large play equipment out. Ten children, two staff. Ricky has made straight for the yellow tractor and is enjoying scooting it down the slope. As he stops to turn back 'uphill', Brendan runs over to ask if he can have a go. Ricky says 'No, I'm on it.' Brendan looks around, sees staff occupied with other children and punches Brendan in the back. Brendan starts to cry, gets off the tractor. Mrs B comforts him but he won't say why he is crying. Brendan scoots off on the tractor.
Action	I talked to Ricky and Brendan together and told them what I saw happen. I explained to Brendan that it was a very unkind thing to do to punch Ricky and something we don't allow in nursery and school. I got him to say 'sorry' to Ricky. Talked to them about 'sharing' - asked how they could share the tractor. All agreed that they would take turns - two goes each before swapping. All staff to keep an eye on the situation and praise both boys when they are seen to be sharing toys and taking turns. Tell Brendan's mum what happened. Review situation next week in staff meeting (date...)

INDIVIDUAL EDUCATION PLAN

NAME:	DoB:	PRE-SCHOOL:

PLAN NO: **ACTION/ACTION PLUS DATE:**

AREA(S) FOR DEVELOPMENT:

TARGETS	STRATEGIES, RESOURCES, CONTRIBUTIONS
1	
2	
3	

TO BE ACHIEVED BY: REVIEW DATE:
SIGNATURES: SENCO: PARENTS/GUARDIANS:

REVIEW
1
2
3

FUTURE ACTION

SIGNATURES: SENCO: PARENTS/GUARDIANS:

INDIVIDUAL EDUCATION PLAN

NAME: *Rehanah*   **DoB:**   **PRE-SCHOOL:** Holly Lane Kindergarten

PLAN NO: **ACTION/ACTION PLUS DATE:**

AREA(S) FOR DEVELOPMENT: *Listening and attention skills*

TARGETS	STRATEGIES, RESOURCES, CONTRIBUTIONS
1 *Rehanah will be able to sit on her own carpet square for a short story once a week with some adult support*	*Rehanah's key worker will sit next to her with a copy of the book being read and will draw Rehanah's attention to the story and pictures – Rehanah could take her carpet square with her to any activity requiring listening*
2 *Rehanah will tell her key worker what the first activity on her personal timetable is every morning and put finished work into the right box with minimal adult support*	*The key worker will go over what the first activity is and prompt Rehanah about what the task is and how she will do it – when it is finished Rehanah will put it into her 'finished' box*
3 *Rehanah will be able to carry out simple instructions 3 out of 4 times*	*Adults will give Rehanah only one instruction at a time whenever they want her to do something – when she has done it, the next instruction will be given. The instruction should be made personal by using Rehanah's name*

TO BE ACHIEVED BY: REVIEW DATE:
SIGNATURES: SENCO: PARENTS/GUARDIANS:

REVIEW
1
2
3

FUTURE ACTION

SIGNATURES: SENCO: PARENTS/GUARDIANS:

INDIVIDUAL EDUCATION PLAN

NAME: *William*   **DoB:**   **PRE-SCHOOL:** Holly Lane Kindergarten

PLAN NO: **ACTION/ACTION PLUS DATE:**

AREA(S) FOR DEVELOPMENT: *Social skills, confidence*

TARGETS	STRATEGIES, RESOURCES, CONTRIBUTIONS
1 *William will play a game with one other child and an adult for a short period every day*	*William's key worker will set this up and provide the language role model and appropriate encouragement*
2 *William will choose the book at story time twice per week when he is asked by his key worker*	*The key worker will explain to William that he is in charge of choosing the story and will give him a reminder beforehand so that he does not feel under pressure*
3	

TO BE ACHIEVED BY: REVIEW DATE:

SIGNATURES: SENCO: PARENTS/GUARDIANS:

REVIEW
1
2
3

FUTURE ACTION

SIGNATURES: SENCO: PARENTS/GUARDIANS:

INDIVIDUAL EDUCATION PLAN – TRACKING SHEET

NAME:		DoB:	DATE:
KEY WORKER:			PRE-SCHOOL:

DATE:	TARGET: (1, 2, OR 3)	COMMENTS:	DATE ACHIEVED:

MEETING WITH PARENTS/CARERS

Pre-school:	**Date:**
Name of child:	

Key worker:

Parent/carer:

Points discussed

Action

Signatures: Parent/carer: Key worker:

APPENDIX 2

Rehanah

ADMISSION

On the admission form completed by the parents for Rehanah's entry into pre-school, there was nothing to indicate that there were any problems. Rehanah started at the pre-school when she was three years and five months old: her mum would have liked her to start sooner but waited until Rehanah was fully toilet trained. She attended pre-school for three sessions each week.

On entry into pre-school, staff noticed straight away that Rehanah was more active than most of the other children. This was particularly evident during the more structured times, for example during snack time and story time. She had difficulty concentrating and flitted from activity to activity, not really playing with anything in particular. She would often climb over other children to reach an object, interrupted adults when they were talking and often talked 'off topic'.

When adults gave instructions to the group as a whole, Rehanah sometimes did what was asked but often appeared to ignore them. She particularly enjoyed pushing a buggy around the hall and would play with this for much of the session, banging into other children and tables.

STAFF DISCUSSION

Rehanah's key worker raised concerns about the child after only two sessions. She talked to the supervisor and SENCO and all agreed that Rehanah needed to be closely observed, but that she may just need an extended settling-in period. It could be that Rehanah had little or no experience of large groups.

OBSERVATION

It was decided to focus on observing Rehanah during story time and during the free play session. This was to gain an impression of how Rehanah behaved in two contrasting situations. Over a period of four weeks, information was gathered about what Rehanah was doing during the story session and what activities she was choosing during the free time session.

STAFF MEETING

The key worker and the SENCO met to discuss Rehanah's progress. Observations indicated that Rehanah was disruptive during every single story session. She constantly shuffled about on her hands and knees, disturbing the children all around her and she shouted out and interrupted the story. During the free play sessions, she invariably chose the buggy, ignoring all the other toys and not allowing other children to share.

ACTION FROM STAFF MEETING
It was decided to focus on the behaviour at story time and also to discuss concerns with mum.

MEETING WITH MUM
Key worker and SENCO spoke to mum who was surprised to find that staff were concerned about Rehanah. The key worker explained that Rehanah had not taken note of what she had said on several occasions and asked mum whether hearing had ever been investigated. It was suggested that Rehanah should be taken to see the GP who could organise a hearing check. The key worker and SENCO discussed some strategies they could use to help Rehanah to sit with the other children during story time. They asked mum if she would mind them contacting the area SENCO for some ideas. Mum agreed with this.

DISCUSSION WITH AREA SENCO
The area SENCO came into the pre-school to discuss some managing strategies based on the information the pre-school gave her. (These strategies are outlined in Case Study 5.) The area SENCO suggested that they focus on one or two strategies over the next few weeks. She also advised that the staff monitored what was working and did more of that. The area SENCO said she would contact the pre-school in about four weeks by phone for feedback.

SECOND MEETING BETWEEN STAFF AND MUM
Prior to this meeting, mum had informed the pre-school that Rehanah's hearing had been checked and found to be normal. The area SENCO had

also contacted the pre-school to see how things were going. She was told that there had not been much progress. The area SENCO offered to help write a more structured programme if mum agreed.

At this meeting, the feedback from the pre-school was that the strategy employed of sitting Rehanah close to an adult while listening in a small group, was not working well enough. Rehanah still poked other children and wandered off. They explained to mum that an area SENCO could come in and help them to write an individual programme. They explained that this meant putting Rehanah's name on the Special Needs Register and working on some very small targets in a more intensive way.

At this meeting, mum mentioned that the health visitor had had some concerns about Rehanah being 'constantly on the go'. Mum seemed happy with the involvement of the area SENCO.

PROVISION (implementation of the plan)
The pre-school SENCO, the key worker and the area SENCO discussed and worked out some targets to go on Rehanah's Individual Education Plan and a recording mechanism (see Appendix 1 for a tracking sheet). This plan was to be shared with all the staff working in the pre-school and closely adhered to. (See Rehanah's Individual Education Plan on page 64)

The area SENCO advised the staff to review the plan after about half a term or before then, if the targets had been met.

REVIEW OF IEP MEETING
The SENCO and the key worker found that working on smaller targets was having more of an impact on Rehanah's behaviour. Targets 1 and 2 were being met and Rehanah could sit on her own for 3 minutes before wandering off. Rehanah continued to have difficulty in carrying out simple instructions. This raised concerns about her understanding . The SENCO and the key worker decided that it could be a good idea to ask mum if they could refer Rehanah to a speech and language therapist. They decided that they would need more help with Target 3 (carrying out simple instructions). When they received some advice they could write a more focused target. It was agreed that the key worker should feed back informally to mum.

MEETING WITH MUM

The key worker had an informal meeting with mum to discuss the above. She explained that the staff didn't know enough about speech and language areas and needed some advice in order to design a proper programme for Rehanah.

Although mum did not fully accept that Rehanah had problems in this area, she agreed to the pre-school staff contacting the speech and language department for advice.

INFORMATION FROM THE SPEECH AND LANGUAGE THERAPIST

The speech and language assessment picked up mild comprehension difficulties and gave the pre-school some ideas they could use in their programme. Included in the report was reference to the fact that Rehanah had proved difficult to assess as she constantly roamed around the room. The speech and language therapist suggested a further assessment to investigate attention difficulties.

ACTION IN THE PRE-SCHOOL

The pre-school continued to work on the Individual Education Plan, targeting listening and attention skills and reviewing them regularly. Rehanah was making better progress in listening and comprehension areas. She continued to have difficulties with attention to task and concentration. After about two terms, the pre-school recommended that Rehanah be assessed by a paediatrician. Mum was beginning to recognise that Rehanah was more difficult to manage at home. She was not listening to instructions and having temper tantrums when she couldn't have her own way.

OUTCOME

Mum decided to become involved in Rehanah's Individual Education Plan. She focused on helping her to develop better listening skills and gradually Rehanah began to follow simple instructions. Mum used appropriate rewards for wanted behaviours and tried not to give Rehanah attention for the temper tantrums.

The paediatrician recognised that Rehanah had some difficulties regarding behaviour, especially concentration and attention, but was reluctant to make a formal diagnosis at this stage. She said she would see Rehanah at regular intervals.

The area SENCO who was supporting the pre-school advised that they should continue to work on small step targets to maintain progress.

TRANSFER INTO SCHOOL
A copy of the Individual Education Plan with reviews was sent to school. A meeting was arranged concerning Rehanah's admission needs. The school recognised the support Rehanah had been given and were in a position to carry on meeting her needs at School Action level of intervention.

Social and emotional development checklist

It is important that any checklist is used with sensitivity. It should not be used to highlight what the child cannot do or to create unrealistic expectations. Instead, it should be seen as a very rough guide to the developmental steps most children take between the ages of two and five.

Age 2–3 years

- Increasing co-operation with parental requests: will *usually* do what is asked

- May prefer to play alongside other children rather than with them

- Finds difficulty in taking turns and sharing

- Needs help to resolve problems with peers, e.g. if another child will not let him play with a toy

- Carries out simple instructions, e.g. bringing or taking objects from room to room

- Sits with adult to share books for five minutes

- Says 'please' and 'thank you' when reminded

- Makes attempts to help parent/carer with chores

- Plays 'dressing up' in adult clothes

- Makes a choice between, e.g. a cake or a biscuit, when asked

- Shows understanding of feeling by verbalising, 'Maddy is hurt – she's crying'

- Shows own feelings such as fear, affection etc.

- Beginning to respond to 'obvious' humour

Age 3–4

- Sings and dances to music

- Imitates other children regarding the following of rules

- May become angry if things don't go his way, but beginning to control feelings – less chance of temper tantrums

- Greets familiar adults without reminder

- Follows rules in adult-led activity

- Asks permission to use a toy being played with by another child

- Increasingly says 'please' and 'thank you' without reminders

- Is able to the answer the telephone and talk to a familiar person

- Will take turns in a game or reaching into biscuit tin etc.

- Co-operates with adult requests 75% of the time

- Stays in own garden/playground area

- Plays near and talks with other children when engaged in own activity

- Often prefers to play with others, wants to please friends

- Likes to dress himself and increasingly tries to be independent

Age 4–5

- Asks for help when having difficulty

- Contributes to adult conversation

- Repeats rhymes, songs or dances

- Is able to work alone at an activity for up to 20 minutes

- Will apologise without a reminder

- Will take turns with an increasingly larger group of children (8 or 9)

- Will play co-operatively with other children, forming small groups that sometimes exclude others

- Shows less physical aggression (hitting others), but uses verbal threats –'I'll kick you, I'll tell my dad'

- Beginning to understand the power of rejection – 'You can't be my friend'

- May lie to avoid getting into trouble – 'It wasn't me!'

- Dresses and eats with minimum supervision

- Engages in socially acceptable behaviour in public

(Adapted from various sources for use with settings in Medway LEA.)

GLOSSARY

autistic spectrum disorder (ASD)	a developmental disorder that is characterised by social and communication difficulties
cognition	how a child thinks and learns
emotional development	the way a child controls and expresses his feelings
expressive language	spoken language, talking
language delay	limited and/or immature use of language
language disorder	a difficulty with the understanding of words and their use
neurological	associated with the brain and nervous system
receptive language	understanding what is said
self-esteem	the way we see ourselves – a child with high self-esteem has a positive picture of himself
social	the way a child relates to his peers and adults and how he is able to respond to systems and organisation
social awareness	the ability to act in an appropriate way in different settings, e.g., organised groups such as pre-school settings
speech disorder	this could be a difficulty with pronouncing single or combined sounds and/or sentence structure
structure	giving structure to an activity or a day's activities means planning and organising things to good effect

FURTHER READING

Barrow, Giles, Emma Bradshaw and Trudie Newton (2001) *Improving Behaviour and Raising Self-Esteem in the Classroom*. London: David Fulton Publishers.

Bender, Pamela Stone (1997) *How to Keep Your Kids from Driving You Crazy: A Proven Programme for Improving Your Child's Behaviour and Regaining Control of Your Family*. Chichester: John Wiley & Sons.

Drifte, Collette (2001) *Special Needs in Early Years Settings: A Guide for Practitioners*. London: David Fulton Publishers.

Fabel, Adele and Elaine Mazlish (1999) *How to Talk so Kids will Listen and Listen so Kids will Talk*. London: Avon Books.

Green, Dr Christopher (1992) *Toddler Taming*. London: Vermillion.

Lear, R. (1996) *Play Helps*. Oxford: Heinemann Educational.

O'Brien, Tim (1998) *Promoting Positive Behaviour*. Essex County Council.

Phelan, Thomas (1995) *1–2–3 Magic: Effective Discipline for Children 2–12 Years*. Glen Ellyn, IL: Child Management Inc.

Roffey, Sue and Terry O'Reirdan (2001) *Young Children and Classroom Behaviour*. London: David Fulton Publishers.

USEFUL ADDRESSES

Down's Syndrome Association
155 Mitcham Road
London SW17 9PG
Tel: 020 8682 4001
Email: info@downs-syndrome.org.uk

National Autistic Society
393 City Road
London EC1V 1NG
Tel: 020 7833 2299
Email: nas@nas.org.uk

OASIS
Office for Advice, Assistance, Support and Information on Special Needs
Helpline: 09068 633201

Parentline Plus
Unit 520
Highgate Studios
53–57 Highgate Road
London NW5 1TL

Pre-school Learning Alliance
69 Kings Cross Road
London WC1X 9LL
Tel: 020 7833 0991

Picture Exchange Communication System
Pyramid Office
226 West Park Place
Newark DE 19711
USA
Tel: 001 888 732 7462
Email: pyramid@pecs.com

Social and Emotional Behaviour Difficulties Association
Church House
1 St Andrews View
Penrith
Cumbria CA11 7YF
Tel: 01768 210510

Sure Start Unit
Level 2
Caxton House
Tothill Street
London SW1H 9NA

DATE DUE
